Your Local Area

SEASIDE

Ruth Thomson

Photography by Neil Thomson

Essex County Council

First published in 2010 by Wayland

This paperback edition published in 2012 by Wayland

Copyright © Wayland 2010

Wayland
338 Euston Road
London NW1 3BH

Wayland Australia
Hachette Children's Books
Level 17/207 Kent Street
Sydney NSW 2000

Editor: Nicola Edwards
Designer: Edward Kinsey
Design Manager: Paul Cherrill

Acknowledgements:
The author and publisher would like to thank
Graham Bennett at Ventnor Heritage Museum
for providing pictures of Ventnor in the past.

British Library Cataloguing in Publication Data

Thomson, Ruth, 1949-
  Your local area.
  Seaside.
  1. Seaside resorts--Juvenile literature. 2. Beaches--
  Juvenile literature. 3. Seashore--Juvenile literature.
  I. Title
  910.9'146-dc22

  ISBN: 978 0 7502 6955 1

Printed in China

Wayland is a division of Hachette Children's Books,
a Hachette UK Company.
www. hachette.co.uk

Free downloadable material is available to complement
the activities in the Your Local Area series, including
worksheets, templates for charts and photographic
identification charts. For more information go to:
www.waylandbooks.co.uk/yourlocalarea
<http://www.waylandbooks.co.uk/yourlocalarea>

Contents

What is the seaside?

The seaside is where land meets the sea. In some places, the land ends at high cliffs. Elsewhere, waves wash over sandy, rocky or shingle beaches.

cliffs

sandy beach

What differences are there between these coasts?

shingle beach

The level of the sea rises up the beach and falls away again twice every day. These movements are called tides.

When the sea comes in, this is called high tide.

When the sea goes out, this is called low tide.

There are many seaside towns. Some were once fishing villages, built on an estuary, the part of a river that meets the sea, or in a sheltered bay. Others were ports with stone-built harbours for ships transporting animals, coal or wool.

Some of the fishermen's cottages are now holiday homes.

This stony bank protects the shore from stormy waves.

The flashing lamp at the top of a lighthouse used to warn sailors about dangers near the coast. Some helped ships find their way safely into harbour. Lighthouses were built on the top of cliffs or on rocks out at sea.

How far is the seaside?

The United Kingdom and Ireland have thousands of miles of coastline and no one lives more than 160 km (100 miles) from the coast. Millions of people visit holiday seaside towns, known as resorts, every year.

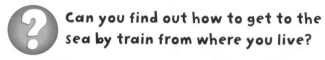

Can you find out how to get to the sea by train from where you live?

A local look

Look at this map showing the most visited seaside resorts in the UK.

★ Which is the nearest resort to where you live?

★ Find out how far the resort is from your home.

★ Look at a road map to find out the quickest way to get there.

Seaside holidays

People visit the seaside for their holidays, especially in summer when the weather is warmest. They enjoy the beach and the sea. Some do water sports, such as sailing and surfing. Others go sea fishing or take walks along the coast and enjoy sea views and the fresh air.

Coastal Path

 What activities are people doing on this beach?

A local look

Seaside resorts are much busier at some times of the year than others.

★ **Make a calendar showing the twelve months of the year.**
★ **Mark on it the months when there are school holidays and half terms.**
★ **Do a class survey to find out which month is most popular for going to the seaside. Which is the least popular?**

Calendar

January	February	March	April
May	June	July	August summer holidays
September	October	November	December

★ **Visit an internet weather site. Choose a seaside resort and see which months last year were the warmest, coldest and rainiest. Mark these on your calendar.**

Staying by the seaside

Some people live at the seaside all year round. Like everyone else, they need homes, shops, schools, hospitals and parks in their local area.

What features do this seaside house and the blocks of flats have in common? Why were they built like this?

A local look

Seaside homes and streets often have a name to do with the sea.

★ **Do the house and street names near your home give any clues about your area?**

PORTVIEW

SEASPRAY COTTAGE

SEAVIEW ST.

ONE TIDES REACH

Thousands of holidaymakers visit seaside resorts all at the same time. Resorts need a large number of places for these extra people to stay.

 Are there any places to stay like these in your local area?

hotel

bed and breakfast

holiday house

self-catering flats

camping and caravan site

There are often camping and caravan sites at the seaside. Some resorts have holiday parks, which have places to stay, swimming pools and all sorts of entertainments. None of these is usually open all year round.

The seafront

The seafront of most seaside towns is lined with places where holidaymakers can stay, eat or drink. The shops mostly sell beach goods, souvenirs or sweets. People walk along and choose where to eat and shop.

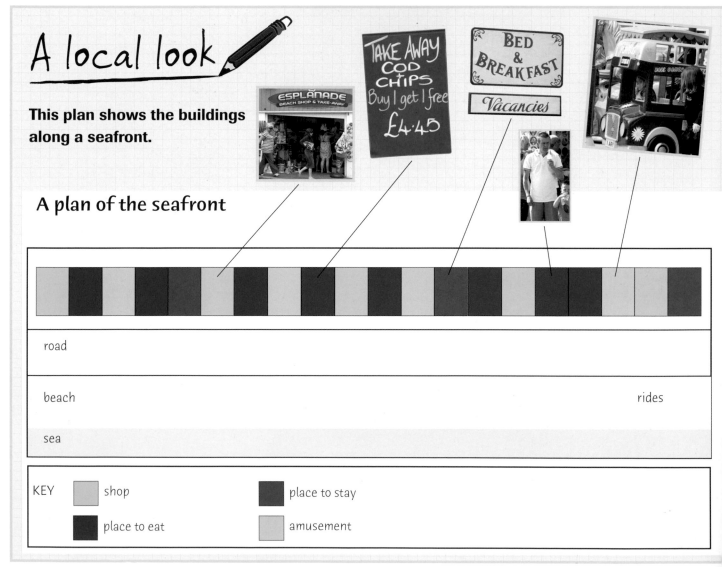

A local look

This plan shows the buildings along a seafront.

A plan of the seafront

road

beach   rides

sea

KEY   □ shop   ■ place to stay

       ■ place to eat   □ amusement

How do shops and cafés attract customers?

rides

★ **Count the places to eat and stay, the shops and amusements along this seafront. Plot your findings on a block graph like this.**

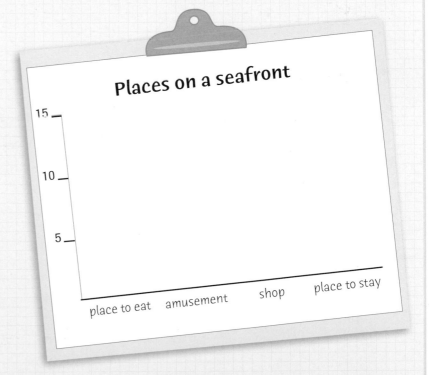

Places on a seafront

15 —

10 —

5 —

place to eat   amusement   shop   place to stay

★ **Why are there many more places to eat than shops?**

The beach

The beach is an open space free to everyone, just like a park. People can sit wherever they like, on the ground or on deckchairs. They can bring picnics, play ball games or run about.

People can paddle, splash or swim in the sea and take rides in canoes or pedalos. On some beaches, you can pay for funfair rides, slides or trampolines.

A local look

★ Are all these activities on the beach free? Which might you have to pay for?
★ Why is a beach a good place for ball games? Why might it not be such a good place?

making sandcastles

surfboarding

digging

rock pooling

canoes and pedalos

paddling

playing music

deckchairs

★ **Make a chart like the one below, comparing activities you can do on a beach or in the sea with activities you can do at your local park or in a swimming pool. How many are the same?**

beach cricket

A comparison of activities

beach or sea	park or pool
🐾 football	🐾 football
🐾 swimming	🐾 swimming
🐾 rock pooling	🐾 skateboarding

Attractions

Seaside towns have more places where you can go for fun than most towns.

The towns want visitors to come all year round, so they often have zoos, fun-fairs, theme parks and indoor swimming pools. These attract people even in bad weather.

Some seaside towns still have donkey rides, sand castle competitions and helter-skelters, which are more old-fashioned fun.

A local look

★ Have you ever visited any attractions like these at the seaside?
★ Which do you think are open all year round and which might open only during the holiday season?

adventure playground

aquarium

★ Which attractions would you go to in bad weather?
★ Which of these attractions do you have in your local area?

boating lake

crazy golf course

indoor play area

multi-screen cinema

big wheel

bouncy castle

★ Find out which of these attractions existed when your parents were children and which ones are newer.

Work

Residents of seaside resorts often work in schools, offices, shops and other places that do not depend on tourists. Some have jobs that help to keep the town looking clean and attractive.

In the busy summer holidays, extra people work in hotels, cafés, shops and seaside attractions. This work is known as seasonal, because people do not work all year round.

? What are these workers doing? What time of year do you think it is?

In summer, there is also all sorts of work on the beach. Lifeguards make sure people in the sea are safe. Other people hire out pedalos, windbreaks and beach huts, or sell ice creams, sweets, snacks and souvenirs.

A local look

Look at these pictures.

★ Make a chart like the one below. List jobs you think people do at the seaside all year round and jobs which are seasonal. How many others can you think of?

beach cleaner

Jobs people do at the seaside

all year round jobs
- postal worker
- police officer

seasonal jobs
- deck chair attendant
- ice cream seller

deckchair attendant

singer at a beach café

postal worker

waitress

fishing tackle shop

Moving around

Seaside towns are full of traffic during holiday times. People want to park as near to the beach as possible. Planners create schemes to help traffic flow smoothly and to provide parking places.

? Which of these parking arrangements do you think is better and why?

A local look

In this town, motorists can park in a car park on the outskirts of town and ride for free into the centre by bus.

The narrow streets of this seaside town were built before cars existed. Traffic flows only one way through the town.

★ How do these schemes help traffic flow at the seaside?

★ What helps traffic flow in your area?

There are different ways to get from one place to another at the seaside.

Funicular railways are a quick way to go up and down a cliff.

Open-top buses take holidaymakers on tours around the sights.

Some seaside towns are built on an estuary. Water taxis and ferries carry passengers from one side to another.

Road trains take visitors for short rides along the seafront.

Victorian resorts

Seaside resorts grew in Victorian times, after railways were built to the coast. Rich families took long holidays. Factory workers could not afford holidays. They only began coming to the seaside for a day out once Bank Holidays started in 1871.

? What do you notice about the clothes these people are wearing at the seaside?

SIGN OF THE PAST

The Victorians built many seaside features that you can still see today.

They built the wide pavement, known as an esplanade or promenade, along the seafront.

In bad weather, people could shelter on covered seats, like this one.

Clock towers were built to celebrate Queen Victoria's long reign.

Many resorts had a long pier that jutted over the sea.
It had a landing stage at the end for paddle steamers
and a pavilion for entertainments.

Rich Victorian families built large
holiday houses called villas. Many
of these are still standing.

Some villas have now been turned
into hotels or guesthouses, or
divided into flats.

Holidays in the past

Holidaymakers in the past enjoyed being on the beach just as they do now. Adults relaxed on deckchairs, while children dug in the sand, paddled in the sea and collected shells. People strolled along the promenade, showing off their best clothes.

 How does the beach scene of the past compare with the same beach today?

People who wanted to swim had to pay for a changing hut on wheels, called a bathing machine. Attendants pushed the machines into the sea and pulled them out again with a winch and chains.

seaside villas

grand hotel on
the promenade

men's bathing
machines

women's bathing
machines on a
separate part of the
beach from men's

Changes in seaside holidays

After the First World War, more and more people started taking holidays at the seaside. People enjoyed boat trips and listening to bands, as well as sitting on the beach and swimming.

In the 1920s and 1930s, groups of workers often travelled for a day out by the sea in open-topped coaches called charabancs.

In the 1950s and 1960s, families started taking a fortnight's seaside holiday. They camped, stayed in a caravan or a guest house or went to a holiday camp. By the 1970s, people started holidaying in warmer countries, such as Spain and France. Some people now have holidays all over the world.

resorts in the 1960s

What attractions were there at these resorts? What did children and adults wear on the beach?

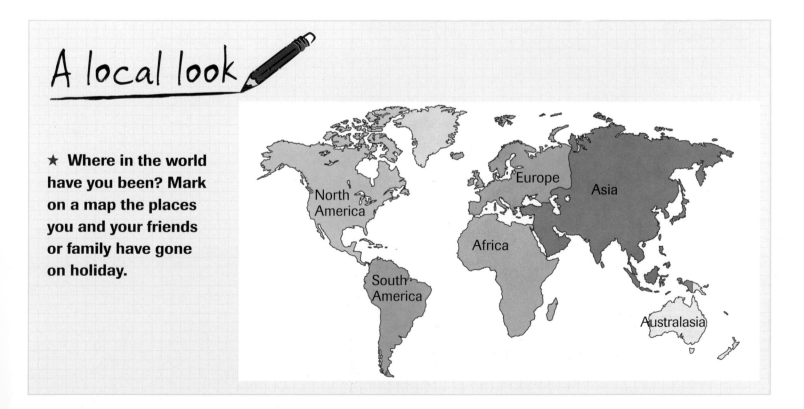

A local look

★ **Where in the world have you been? Mark on a map the places you and your friends or family have gone on holiday.**

North America

South America

Europe

Asia

Africa

Australasia

More things to do

★ Collect leaflets that tell tourists about attractions at seaside resorts. You can find these from the tourist offices or download them from the Internet.

★ Notice the words that leaflets use to attract visitors, such as: *new, fun, exciting, beautiful, thrilling, magical, all weather, explore* and *enjoy.*

★ Make a brochure to attract visitors to your own area, describing any special features.

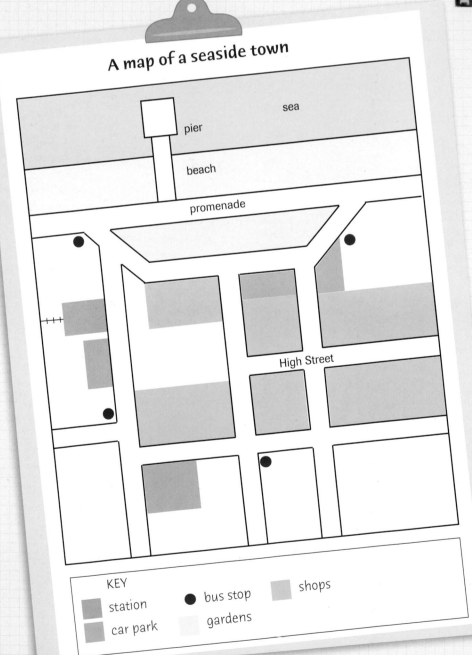

A map of a seaside town

sea

pier

beach

promenade

High Street

KEY

■ station

● bus stop

■ shops

■ car park

gardens

★ Compare this map of the seaside with a map of your area.

★ Notice how many roads lead down to the sea.

★ Notice how the main shopping streets are set back from the beach.

★ How many car parks does your area have compared with this resort?

★ **Look for postcards that show landmarks or special features of a seaside town.**

★ **Ask your family if they have kept any old postcards, so you can compare them with modern ones.**

★ **Design your own postcard and write a message on the back.**

★ **Find out what sort of souvenirs people bring back from their holidays.**

★ **What are they made from?**

★ **Are they reminders of a particular resort or do they just remind you of the sea?**

★ **Ask older people what souvenirs they used to buy when they were young.**

wooden boat

ceramic fish

granite ornament

sugar rock

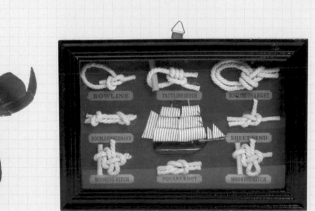

plastic crab

sailors' knots

shell yacht

Glossary

amusement a machine or activity that people can enjoy

attraction something people want to do or see, such as a zoo

Bank Holiday one of several weekdays (usually Mondays) in the year when banks, shops and factories are officially closed

bay an area of land on the shore that bends inwards

beach the area of sand or pebbles that has been left on the shore by the tides

cliff a high, steep rocky slope facing the sea

coast the area of land next to the sea

estuary the widest part of a river which runs into the sea

harbour a place on the coast protected from wind and rough waves, where boats can dock and shelter

lifeguard someone who works on a beach to rescue people in difficulties in the sea

pavilion a large, bright building for entertainments

pier a long, high platform built over the sea, where people can walk and ships could tie up

port a place where ships can load or unload goods or shelter in bad weather

promenade a wide pavement or path built along a seafront for people to walk

resident someone who lives in a place

resort a seaside place where people go on holiday

shore the strip of land beside the sea or a lake

souvenir something people buy to remind them of a particular place

tide the twice-daily rise and fall of the sea

Victorian the time when Queen Victoria ruled Britain – from 1837 to 1901

villa a large house

wave a moving ridge of water in the sea

windbreak something that protects people from the force of the wind

?Talking points

The questions in the book encourage close observation of the pictures and provide talking points for discussion.

Pages 4-5
Cliffs are made of rock, such as sandstone, chalk, limestone or clay. Shingle beaches are made up of rocks, which have been worn by the sea into smooth pebbles. Sand is made of rocks or shells, which have been ground by the sea, over millions of years into tiny grains.

Pages 6-7
The oldest seaside resorts, such as Blackpool, Southend and Brighton, are those close to large cities, which had railways connecting them. Until the 1960s, many more resorts were connected to the railway than today.

Pages 8-9
There are people relaxing, eating or reading on the sand or in deckchairs, making a sandcastle and paddling in the sea.

Pages 10-11
• Both the house and block of flats have large windows and balconies, so inhabitants can enjoy sitting looking at the sea.
• Notice how the height of the block of flats is stepped down to allow the older houses on the cliff above to still have a sea view.
• Much new housing by the sea is blocks of flats rather than houses, because there is so little spare land.

Pages 12-13
• There are more places to eat because people like a choice of things to eat and drink and do not want to have to walk very far from the beach. There are different types of food and drink shops on a seafront – some sell takeaway food and drink, some are cafés where people can sit down for a drink, snack or a meal, some sell rock, fudge and other sweets as souvenirs.
• Shops attract customers with colourful shop fronts, decorated with what they sell. These two shops also have signboards on the pavement which shoppers can spot from a distance.

Pages 14-15
• People have to pay to hire deck chairs, canoes and pedalos – all the other activities shown are free.
• People also have to pay for a turn on a trampoline, for funfair and donkey rides. They also pay to hire deckchairs, windbreaks, umbrellas and beach huts, if they do not have their own.

Pages 16-17
• Cinemas, indoor play areas and adventure playgrounds are open all year round. Boating lakes, funfairs, crazy golf and bouncy castles are open only in the holiday season.
• Indoor attractions, such as an aquarium, an indoor play area and a cinema are popular in bad weather.

Pages 18-19
• These workers are painting the railings along a promenade to improve the look of the resort. They work in the spring, before the main holiday season starts.
• The lifeguard works only in the summer season, when hundreds of holidaymakers have fun in the sea and some may get into difficulties.

Pages 20-21
• The car park (top picture) confines cars to one part of the beach, but means that people may have further to walk. The car parking along the length the esplanade (bottom picture) may be more convenient for people who want to use a particular stretch of beach, but spoils the look of the seafront.
• The one-way system along narrow roads allows cars to flow smoothly around town without needing to stop and give way to drivers coming from the opposite direction. The double yellow lines mean no parking, which helps the traffic flow more easily.

Pages 22-23
• The people are wearing their best clothes. Some of the men are wearing suits and ties. Most people are wearing a hat, including some of the children. The man's flat straw hats are called boaters. The little boy in the foreground is wearing a sailor suit, a fashion made popular by Queen Victoria's eldest son.

Pages 24-25
• The beach scene of 1907 is much more cluttered with bathing machines and their winches, rowing boats, huts and stripy tents.
• The modern beach has a clear expanse of sand with wooden huts and a flag to show the safe areas for bathing. There are railings along the edge of the promenade. The modern promenade has a road for cars, which hardly existed when the old picture was taken.

Pages 26-27
• The 1960s attractions are boat rides, funfair rides, walks along the seafront gardens and the pier. Children could research on the internet what attractions today's resorts offer to compete with holiday resorts overseas.
• The two women are wearing bikinis, first introduced in the 1950s. The children wear one-piece swimsuits.

Index